BIRDS
of PREY

BIRDS
of PREY

PAUL D. FROST

p

This is a Parragon Publishing Book

First published in 2006

Parragon Publishing
Queen Street House
4 Queen Street
Bath BA1 1HE, UK

Designed, produced, and packaged by Stonecastle Graphics Limited

Text by Paul D. Frost
Edited by Philip de Ste. Croix
Designed by Paul Turner and Sue Pressley

ISBN 1-40547-131-X

Printed in China

PIEBALD EAGLE

Page 1: The very distinctive white head of the Bald Eagle (*Haliaeetus leucocephalus*) is only fully developed at seven years old. Juvenile Bald Eagles have brown heads which turn to a mottled color as the bird matures, before finally whitening. It is possible that the name Bald Eagle derives from a contraction of 'piebald' meaning 'brown and white,' or possibly from the Old English word 'balde' meaning white.

IN FOR THE KILL

Pages 2 and 3: Snowy Owls (*Bubo scandiacus*) prey mainly on small rodents, in particular lemmings and voles. Hunting is often done from a suitably high perch, which affords the owls a good view over the usually bleak terrain of the Arctic tundra which is their natural habitat. Prey is usually caught from above following the owl's silent gliding approach from its perch.

CONTENTS

INTRODUCTION
Page 6

EAGLES AND OSPREY
Page 14

HAWKS
Page 32

FALCONS
Page 50

VULTURES
Page 66

OWLS
Page 76

INDEX
Page 96

INTRODUCTION

This book not only sets out to inform its readers about a wide variety of birds of prey – the aerial predators of the world – it is also beautifully illustrated with many pictures which portray these impressive birds in their natural habitats in the wild.

Firstly, it is necessary to explain exactly what a bird of prey is. One dictionary definition suggests 'any of numerous carnivorous birds that hunt and kill other animals.' However, there are many carnivorous birds, such as the kingfisher family, that are not birds of prey. The feature that distinguishes carnivorous birds that are considered 'birds of prey' from all the others is the method by which they catch and kill their prey. Birds of prey use the sharp talons of their feet as their primary method of killing their prey, whereas other carnivorous birds tend to use only their beaks for this task.

Another term often used for birds of prey is 'raptor.' This comes from the Latin word *rapere*, meaning to seize and carry off. Sometimes the term is restricted to the diurnal (daytime hunting) birds of prey, such as eagles and hawks; however, this book accepts the more general definition, as given by the *Oxford English Dictionary*, which also includes owls.

When describing birds of prey, many exceptions crop up which make generalizations difficult. One of the first exceptions that we encounter concerns the definition of raptors using their feet to kill their prey. The

HIGH FLYING BIRD

The Rüppell's Vulture (*Gyps rueppellii*) holds the world record for being the highest flying bird. Unfortunately for the bird in question, it achieved this recognition by colliding with a commercial aircraft. The plane survived and the pilot recorded the height of the event – 37,000 feet (11,300m). The dead vulture was identified from feathers which had stuck to the aircraft.

PREVIOUS PAGES

Page 6: Tawny Eagle (*Aquila rapax*).
Page 7: Osprey (*Pandion haliaetus*).

vultures are predominantly carrion eaters, not killing their prey at all but feeding on the leftovers of other animals (though there are exceptions!), but they are still classified as birds of prey. Also, it is interesting to note that the vultures of North and South America are not related to any of the other birds of prey, but they are nevertheless considered as birds of prey for convenience and historical reasons. The definition also states that birds of prey are carnivorous, despite the fact that there is actually a vegetarian bird of prey, the Palmnut Vulture. The hawks and falcons are often classified as diurnal birds of prey, but there are some exceptions to this definition too. Generally female birds of prey are larger and more aggressive than the males, although again there are some species where this is not the case.

One thing that all birds of prey do have in common is remarkable eyesight. It is estimated that their eyesight is up to ten times better than ours. They are able to see in far more detail than we can and their eyesight is also far more sensitive to movement. Most of the diurnal raptors are believed to be able to distinguish color and some species can see a wider range of colors than humans, some well into the ultra-violet region of the spectrum.

All birds of prey have very sensitive hearing, though this feature is much more pronounced in owls than it is in diurnal raptors. Owls, more so than most of the other birds of prey, rely on sound to locate their prey. Their bodies and senses are specially adapted to help them achieve this goal.

The breeding and nesting habits of the different types of raptor make fascinating study. Many birds of prey mate for life, but there is rarely any sentiment governing this attachment. When one partner dies, it is not unusual for the remaining partner to start searching for a replacement mate within hours. They also exhibit very little attachment to their young. At an early age, sometimes only a matter of weeks after hatching, the young are seen by their parents as competitors for food and so they need to become fully independent very quickly.

Hunting techniques vary enormously. We are used to thinking of birds of prey as excellent fliers, soaring high and stooping and tirelessly chasing their prey on the wing. While some prefer the soaring and quartering techniques involving sustained flight, many raptors are not actually prepared to put that much effort into getting their food. Some favor 'still hunting' – sitting still on a suitable perch, waiting for the

THE EYES HAVE IT

All raptors have remarkable eyesight. Owls, such as this young Spotted Eagle Owl (*Bubo africanus*), can see much better than we can in very low light conditions, aided by a reflective layer behind the retina in the eye which acts to reflect light back onto the retina.

PREENING OSPREY

The Osprey (*Pandion haliaetus*) has a highly developed preen gland near the base of its tail which contains a waterproof oil. It is important that Ospreys have highly waterproofed feathers as they often submerge themselves fully when catching fish, and regular preening maintains this water-resistant coating.

THE DEVIL RIDES OUT

Opposite below: Though often seen walking gracefully, Secretarybirds (*Sagittarius serpentarius*) will frequently lower their heads when hunting and put on a high-speed chase for prey. In some areas of Africa the Secretarybird is more commonly known as 'The Devil's Horse.'

prey to come within easy reach. Others prefer 'perch hunting,' making short flights between suitable perches looking for prey in flight.

There are over 300 different species of diurnal raptor and over 200 species of owl. As current taxonomical studies of raptors evolve, using new techniques, especially DNA analysis, the numbers of recognized species is regularly changing, as is their classification. Often the different techniques of classification give conflicting results, so different authorities will disagree on what constitutes a true species.

When asked to list the various types of birds of prey, most people would answer eagles, hawks, falcons, vultures, and owls. As this book does not set out to be a definitive guide to birds of prey and their taxonomical classification, the birds are here presented in those popularly recognized groups.

Only two species and one family of birds do not easily fit into these groups. The Osprey, though not an eagle, very much resembles one, so it is included in that section. The caracaras are truly members of the falcon family, but they are so different from typical falcons that it does not seem appropriate to include them in that section. Consequently, the caracaras and the Secretarybird are treated separately in this introductory section.

Secretarybird

The Secretarybird is a very distinctive bird only found in Africa, in the grass plains and savannah south of the Sahara. It is the only bird of prey with predominantly terrestrial habits, walking anywhere up to 20 miles (32km) in a day. Despite rarely flying, Secretarybirds are actually very accomplished fliers when they need to be, using thermals to gain height and then soaring for great distances.

The main diet of Secretarybirds is snakes, lizards, grasshoppers, mice, birds' eggs, and the occasional small mammal. Accurately aiming a rear talon at the skull, the Secretarybird usually kills its prey with a very powerful stamp. Their height of over 4ft (1.2m) also enables them to kill some prey by repeatedly picking the creature up and dropping it onto hard ground. Often found at the edges of bush and grass fires, they will prey on anything that is fleeing to escape the flames, frequently also feeding on the carrion that has failed to escape.

Secretarybirds will usually mate for life. Once paired, they normally remain very close together, rarely straying out of one another's sight, although they do sometimes hunt in different areas. Their nests are normally built on the tops of tall trees, with both birds sharing the nesting responsibilities. The nests can be anywhere from 3 to 8ft (1-2.4m) in diameter and are very shallow. Females usually lay a clutch of up to three eggs. When the young birds hatch, unlike the majority of raptors, they exhibit no sibling rivalry, so if two eggs hatch, then both young are likely to survive.

I JUST FLUTTER MY EYELASHES

In addition to a third, inner, translucent eyelid (called the nictitating membrane) which helps to protect its eyes, the Secretarybird's eyelids are adorned with these remarkably long black eyelashes.

Caracas

Nine species of caracara are generally recognized. They are often called 'carrion hawks.' They are found from Florida down to the Falkland Islands and Tierra del Fuego in the southern latitudes. They inhabit the various different environments of South America. The Red-throated Caracara lives deep in the tropical forests. The White-throated Caracara has been seen feeding high in the Andes alongside Andean Condors. The Striated Caracara is to be seen on the rocky coast of the Falkland Islands and other islands in the vicinity. The mostly widely distributed of the family, the Crested Caracara, is found in open countryside and on cattle-ranchland.

Despite being totally different in many ways, including appearance, flying style, diet, and behavior, they are very close relations of falcons.

The caracaras are characterized by their long necks and their yellow to reddish bare cheeks. They are very gregarious and aggressive. They are also very intelligent.

They spend much of the time scavenging on the ground, feeding mainly on carrion. They will eat reptiles, amphibians, and small birds, and the smaller species will eat insects. Though often seen near farms, Crested Caracaras more often than not feed on insects, grubs, and carrion, though some have developed the habit of attacking young livestock. In the late 1800s the Guadalupe Caracara also exhibited this characteristic, and this bird has the distinction of being one of the few species to be deliberately exterminated by man by the early 20th century.

Caracaras tend to nest either high in trees or on rocky ledges, though the Crested Caracara has been known to build nests on the ground or in cactuses.

EAGLES AND OSPREY

These are the most majestic of all of the birds of prey, and eagles are often referred to as the 'King of Birds.' They are the largest in stature of the typical birds of prey family, exceeded in size only by some of the vultures. The eagle has been widely accepted as a symbol of nobility throughout history.

What actually is an eagle? It is not an easy question to answer precisely. The term eagle is used to refer to a very diverse group of large birds of prey. The renowned authority on raptors, Dr. Leslie Brown, once humorously remarked that 'an eagle is a large or very large diurnal raptor which is *not* a kite, buzzard, vulture, hawk or falcon.'

Very similar to the buzzard (buteo) family of raptor, eagles are generally larger, though sometimes not significantly so. Eagles tend to be much more powerfully built than buzzards, regardless of their size. Like buzzards, they have broad rounded wings and a wide rounded tail, but they have larger feet and a much heavier beak. In flight, they are much more ponderous than buzzards and rely more on surprise to catch their prey, rather than pursuit.

Most eagles build their nests in trees, though in regions with very few trees, or where they are only small, the nest sites are likely to be on high mountain crags. The nest site is usually found on an elevated vantage point allowing the eagle to sweep into and out of it with ease. It is not unusual for a pair of eagles to have several nests within their territory, which are used in rotation. Where different species live in the same locality, it has been observed that occasionally an eagle of a different species will use an unoccupied nest within its territory.

NEST WITH A VIEW

Bald Eagles (*Haliaeetus leucocephalus*) almost always build their nests in tall trees near to open water. However, in the very northern reaches of their territory on the small Alaskan islands where trees are in short supply, they will build nests on the ground.

With the exception of the snake eagles, which make relatively small nests, eagles' nests tend to be large, fabricated from sticks and lined with leaves and other suitable soft warm material. Most of the nest building tends to be done by the female. Very often the nests are used from year to year, and each year new material is added both to the structure and the lining of the nests. One of the largest nests on record was made by a pair of Bald Eagles. It measured 10ft (3m) across and was 23ft (7m) high and weighed nearly two tons.

The average clutch size for the majority of eagles is two, but some, especially the larger eagles, lay only a single egg in any year. Incubation is performed mainly by the female, though the males will often share the job. Incubation takes around six weeks on average. If more than one egg is laid and hatched, it is not unusual for the older chick to kill, and even eat, the younger chick. Even if this doesn't happen, the older chick tends to be more strident in its call for food and consequently it gets a greater amount, growing faster and more strongly than its younger sibling.

The period of time before the young are fully fledged is, to a large extent, related to the size of the birds. Little Eagles are fully fledged in around seven to eight weeks on average, while harpy eagles take anywhere up to six months. The young are fully independent of their parents anywhere from a month after fledging up to more than a year in the case of young Philippine Eagles.

There are currently 68 species of raptor that are classified as eagles. Some authorities attempt to classify them into four main groups – true (or booted) eagles, fish (or sea) eagles, snake eagles, and harpy eagles.

True Eagles

This group consists of 32 species, including the smallest of all the eagles, the aptly named Little Eagle, found in Australia, which weighs less than 2lb (900g). They are often referred to as booted eagles, because their legs are thickly feathered all the way down to their toes, unlike most other eagles and buzzards.

CAMP FOLLOWER

The Tawny Eagle (*Aquila rapax*) usually feeds on fresh carrion, often the kills of other raptors, including mammals up to the size of rabbits. It will also hunt for small rodents, lizards and snakes, as well as locusts and grasshoppers. Tawny Eagles are often seen in the vicinity of hunting camps and they may follow hunting and shooting parties in the quest for food. They will boldly swoop down and snatch dead or injured prey before the hunters can collect it. The Indian Tawny Eagle (*Aquila rapax vindhiana*) is pictured below.

Opposite: Bald Eagles become most vocal around the breeding season but, despite their impressive size, they have rather weak voices. Lowering their heads and opening their beaks wide, the call that emerges sounds more like the cries of gulls.

SALMON LEAP

Below: In winter in North America, Bald Eagles often congregate in large flocks along coasts and rivers to take advantage of the abundance of spawning salmon and other fish. Despite the quantity of prey that is available at this time, Bald Eagles will still try to steal food from one another and from Ospreys.

The largest eagle in this group is also the largest eagle in Africa – it is the Martial Eagle, weighing up to 15lb (7kg). The best known of the true eagles is the Golden Eagle. It is found throughout much of the northern hemisphere and is remarkable in its range which extends from the frozen Arctic regions of Alaska down to the hot mountainous lands of the northern Sahara.

True eagles will feed on a variety of prey, including medium-sized birds and mammals ranging in size from rabbits and hares upward. Larger birds are able to catch and kill prey the size of a young deer or antelope. If available, they will also feed on carrion.

Fish Eagles

This group of ten eagles are all predominantly fish-eating. Unlike Ospreys, which are prepared to submerge themselves to catch their prey, fish eagles normally catch a fish by snatching it from near the surface of the water.

The best known of all this group is the Bald Eagle, the largest of the American eagles. It is found throughout most of continental North America, from Alaska through Canada and down to the southern states of the USA. As the national bird of the United States, it is recognized throughout the world. It is the archetypal eagle with large powerful wings, feet, and beak and an impressive noble appearance.

The largest of this group is Steller's Fish Eagle, found in eastern Asia. Females may grow to 44in (1.1m) in length with a wingspan of up to 96in (2.4m), with males being a little smaller. Steller's Fish Eagle is only marginally smaller in size than the Harpy Eagle, but is comparable in terms of its weight and wingspan.

Most of the fish eagles have varying amounts of white on their undersides; this affords them a large degree of camouflage when they are flying low over the water.

Snake Eagles

This group of 22 eagles are characterized by having a diet that predominantly consists of snakes. They are found mainly in Africa, India, China, and Indonesia, but the Short-toed Snake Eagle is migratory and spends summer throughout much of southern and northeastern Europe and parts of Russia.

In addition to snakes, they will also feed on lizards, frogs and other reptiles, small mammals, and occasionally crabs and fish. Most of the food is caught by the technique of 'still hunting,' with the birds often sitting on a partially covered branch by a river clearing, and dropping straight down on snakes as they pass underneath.

MONKEY EATER

At approximately 40in (1m) in height, the Philippine Eagle (*Pithecophaga jefferyi*) is the tallest, though not the largest, of the world's eagles. They mainly prey on large mammals, such as flying lemurs and macaque monkeys, and, because of this, they were previously known as the Monkey-eating Eagle. These impressive raptors often hunt monkeys cooperatively – one bird will distract the troop from the front while another picks off prey at the rear of the group. The Philippine Eagle is now close to extinction due to loss of habitat as a result of intensive agriculture.

Harpy Eagles

This group of eagles consists of four species, which are the largest of all the eagles. The Harpy Eagle and the Crested Eagle are found in parts of Central and South America. The Philippine Eagle and the New Guinea Eagle inhabit the areas that their names suggest.

The world's largest eagle is the Harpy Eagle, which can weigh up to 20lb (9kg). A very close second is the Philippine Eagle, previously known as the Monkey-eating Eagle.

All four are forest-dwelling. They have relatively short, but extremely powerful, wings. They are able to lift and carry off prey that weigh almost as much as they do. They prey on large birds, forest-living mammals (including monkeys), and reptiles. In inhabited regions, they will take domestic livestock – Philippine Eagles have been reported as preying on young pigs and dogs from native villages.

Osprey

The Osprey is not considered as an eagle because in taxonomic terms it occupies a niche all of its own, apparently diverging from the rest of the birds of prey around 24-30 million years ago. However, because it looks and behaves very much like some of the typical fish-eating eagles, it would be capricious not to include it here.

The Osprey is found throughout much of the world, with the exception of central USA, northern Africa, and parts of southern Europe. It tends to breed only in northerly areas.

Ospreys prey almost exclusively on live fish, both saltwater and freshwater. They will only rarely take dead or dying fish. Unlike some other birds of prey, they are very unlikely to try to steal food from other birds, but occasionally their own catches are stolen by other birds, including herons.

Sometimes they locate their prey by 'still-hunting' from a perch, but more often they will glide and soar over a body of water, starting high and coming lower with each swoop. Once they have identified their prey, it will be caught with a feet-first dive, sometimes from a hover but more often from a glide. It is not unusual for an Osprey to submerge itself completely beneath the water to catch its prey, unlike fish eagles that just skim the surface. Some young Osprey can get into difficulty once submerged, lacking the strength to rise out of the water. As the Osprey flies off, it will usually adjust the position of the fish in its talons so that it comes out of the water head first – this reduces the drag of the water on the fish. Fish eagles, on the other hand, tend to bring the fish out sideways, holding it in both feet.

In order to get a better grip on slippery fish, the outermost toe of each foot is reversible and the undersides of the toes and feet are very scaly being covered with small sharp spicules (spines), which enable them to carry off prey weighing as much as 4lb (1.8kg).

Ospreys start to breed at three years old. They build their nests in the tops of trees (usually coniferous, if available), on rocky pinnacles or on artificial platforms. The nests are reused in subsequent years, being added to and relined, and as a consequence they can become very large. The normal clutch size is two or three eggs and incubation takes around five to six weeks. The young are fully fledged at around seven to eight weeks after hatching and they are independent of their parents within two months.

In the first year, up to 60 percent of the young population may die but those that do survive can usually live for 15 to 20 years. Some have been known to live for over 30 years.

FROM THE GROUND UP

Ospreys (*Pandion haliaetus*) construct their large nests by starting with a base of branches and very large twigs. Once the structure is complete, it is lined with any softer material that can be found locally, such as seaweed, reeds, grass, or heather.

LONE STALKER

Left: Golden Eagles (*Aquila chrysaetos*) use a variety of hunting techniques to catch their prey including soaring and stooping, 'still hunting,' and slow, low-level quartering. They have sometimes even been seen stalking slower-moving prey on the ground, approaching cautiously before jumping and grabbing the creature in their talons.

ELECTRIFYING

Above: In some areas of the USA one of the biggest threats to Golden Eagles is electrocution. Their wingspan can exceed 80in (2m). When gliding from electricity pylons their wings are wide enough to span a pair of cables, resulting in them suffering a massive electric shock. Some electricity companies have made modifications to their installations reducing deaths caused in this way by up to 95 percent.

THE REIGN IN SPAIN

Although adult Imperial Eagles
(*Aquila heliaca*) remain resident in
Spain throughout the year, juveniles
migrate to northern Africa for the
winter. Now seriously threatened,
conservation efforts had increased
numbers from 30 breeding pairs in
the late 1970s to 150 pairs by the
early 1990s. However, by the end of
the century numbers were in decline
again. The main causes of this
worrying trend are the use of agro-
chemicals, collision with power lines,
and illegal poisoning.

COLONIAL SUCCESS

The Wedge-tailed Eagle (*Aquila audax*) is found throughout Australia, including its desert regions. They often nest in densely forested regions, but hunt in open countryside. Forest clearing and the introduction of rabbits and sheep from the 19th century onward following the colonization of Australia proved highly beneficial to this eagle. Despite having been one of the world's most persecuted eagles – considered as vermin and with a price on its head in the 1950s – the population is believed to be higher now than it was before colonization.

AMERICAN ICON

In 1784 Benjamin Franklin reported his dismay at the Bald Eagle (*Haliaeetus leucocephalus*) being chosen as the national emblem of the USA. In his view it was a *'bird of bad moral character'* that did *'not get his living honestly.'* He observed that the Bald Eagle was too lazy to fish for itself, preferring to steal from other birds. He also noted that the Bald Eagle is a *'rank coward,'* often being driven out of its territory by the little King Bird, which is no bigger than a sparrow. He went on to extol the virtues of the Turkey as a *'much more respectable bird'* and a *'true original Native of America.'*

Most of the diurnal raptors, such as the Bald Eagle, have a pronounced bony ridge above their eyes, known as the 'supraorbital ridge.' This feature acts as a sun shade, reducing glare to give them a better view of any prey that may be present below.

GAINING A TOE HOLD

Ospreys (*Pandion haliaetus*) will catch large fish of up to 4.5lb (2kg) in weight, often as a result of a stoop from a hover directly above the surfacing fish. Ospreys' feet are highly adapted to holding onto their prey. They have spiky scales on the underside of the talons, but, more importantly, all of the toes are the same length and the outer toe on each foot is reversible to ensure a very secure grip.

HAWKS

The term 'hawk' is used by most people to refer to those raptors that do not fit into the categories of eagle, falcon, vulture, or owl. The term covers a variety of both broad-winged birds of prey, such as the buzzards, kites, and harriers, and also the short-winged true hawks. These are very wide-ranging groups that vary significantly in hunting styles and types of prey.

Buzzards

There are 48 species of raptor that fall into this category, of which 28 are the true buzzards, often referred to as buteos. Typically buzzards are fairly large birds, though, on the whole, they are slightly smaller than eagles. Like eagles, they have very large, broad wings.

Most often seen in soaring flight in search of their prey, in order to gain height they will often search out thermals, rising on currents of warm air. By locking out their big broad wings, they can gain a lot of height, spiraling up in the thermals. The other main style of hunting employed by the buteos is 'still hunting.' Prey consists of small to medium-sized mammals, reptiles, amphibians, invertebrates, and large insects.

The largest of the family is the Ferruginous Hawk that is found throughout much of the western United States. Some weigh over $2^{1}/_{2}$lb (1.1kg). The smallest is the Roadside Hawk weighing only 12oz (340g).

THE WAITING GAME

Although very capable aerial hunters, Red-tailed Hawks (*Buteo jamaicensis*) spend much of their time 'still hunting.' They perch high above the ground, intently inspecting the terrain around them as they wait for prey to come into sight and then swoop down to catch it. They feed mainly on small mammals, but are capable of taking hares weighing as much as 4.5lb (2kg).

PREVIOUS PAGES

Page 32: The Common Buzzard (*Buteo buteo*) is often mistaken for an eagle.
Page 33: The Roadside Hawk (*Rupornis magnirostris*) is found from Mexico down to northern Argentina, and it is the most common hawk found in those regions.

The most common of the buteos encountered in the USA is the Red-tailed Hawk. It is found throughout all areas of the United States, ranging from Central America, Cuba, Jamaica and the other large Caribbean islands all the way up through Canada to Alaska. Almost as large as the Ferruginous Hawk, it is a very aggressive, powerful hunter. Totally unconcerned by living in close proximity to man, these hawks are often found near farms, where they are often called 'Chicken Hawk.' They also live in more urban areas and have even been seen nesting in Central Park, New York.

Buteos usually build their own nests rather than inhabiting the disused nests of other birds. Nests are most often situated in trees but sometimes they are found on cliff edges. Very occasionally birds living in urban areas, such as the Red-tailed Hawk, will nest on man-made structures, such as skyscrapers. The nests are often used in subsequent years, being added to each year. The average clutch size is two or three eggs, but some birds will lay up to five when food is plentiful.

Very closely related to the buzzard family is the Harris' Hawk. In appearance it has the large broad wings that are typical of buzzards, but also the long legs that are characteristic of true hawks. In fact, its Latin family name, *Parabuteo*, means 'like a buzzard.'

Most raptors prefer either solitary hunting or, especially during the breeding season, hunting with their mate. However, the Harris' Hawk will very often hunt co-operatively in quite large, often family-based, groups.

Kites

There are 19 different species in the kite family. While it is known throughout most of the world, only two species are found in North America. The White-tailed Kite is resident in parts of South Carolina and California, while the Mississippi Kite is found in very localized areas of Kansas, Iowa, Tennessee, South Carolina, and Florida.

It is thought that kites are the oldest of the diurnal birds of prey from which all the others evolved. Part of the evidence for this theory comes from the fact that more predatory forms tend to evolve from less predatory forms – kites are the least predatory of the birds of prey. Kites feed mostly on carrion which is supplemented by snails, slugs, and earthworms. When kites prey on birds and mammals, it is often the very young or injured that are taken, rather than fit, healthy adults.

Soaring and low-level gliding, followed by very fast, agile swoops are the main techniques of predation used by kites. Large, broad wings coupled with relatively light body mass aid this style of searching and snatching carrion, which is often eaten on the wing.

The largest of the kites is the Red Kite, which breeds throughout much of Spain, France, Southern Italy, and in localized parts of the UK.

STREET CLEANER

In Britain during the Middle Ages the Red Kite (*Milvus milvus*) was a vital aid to public hygiene, feeding on garbage lying around towns and cities before it rotted, and so it was legally protected. As a result, the kite population grew to such numbers that they eventually needed to prey on domestic livestock for survival. In the 16th century the government declared that Red Kites were vermin and ordered that they should be killed throughout England and Wales.

FEARLESS THIEVES

The Black Kite (*Milvus migrans*) is a very bold scavenger with virtually no fear of humans. Black Kites often live in large numbers around towns and villages where they feed on discarded trash. In Africa and India they are regularly seen in market places swooping down and stealing food from cooking pots and even out of people's hands.

By the 19th century it was close to extinction in Britain, but a campaign started at the time and much revived in recent years involving the introduction of new stock from mainland Europe has seen the population grow back to viable levels. Unfortunately, there is still some persecution of these birds in some quarters. The kite is a carrion eater, but when the bird is seen eating a dead animal, it is wrongly assumed that the kite killed it. So instances of deliberate poisoning still go on, in spite of education campaigns to eliminate this practice.

The smallest of the kites is the Pearl Kite, which weighs less than 4oz (110g). It is found throughout tropical South America.

In terms of numbers, the most successful of all of the birds of prey is the Black Kite. With the exception of the UK, northern Scandinavia, northern Africa, and the Americas, it is found throughout the world. The Black Kite has no fear of man, often living in close proximity to humans and stealing food directly from people's plates. They will scavenge for food around garbage tips on the outskirts of settlements and even follow fishing boats, snatching fish that rise to the surface or are thrown overboard.

Kites usually build their own nests in trees and shrubs, and occasionally on rocky ledges or old buildings. Sometimes a nest will be constructed upon an old disused nest site. Clutch size on average is up to three eggs. Up to ten weeks can elapse before the young are fully fledged and they can remain dependent on their parents for a further ten weeks.

Very closely related to kites are the honey buzzards. Despite their name, honey buzzards feed mainly on the larvae of bees and wasps dug out of the nests or hives, rather than on honey itself. To shield themselves from stings, their faces are covered with a protective layer of small, very tightly packed feathers.

The most widespread of the five species is the Western Honey Buzzard, which is found in the UK and throughout Europe, southern Scandinavia, Russia, and parts of Asia. It is a highly migratory bird, overwintering in sub-Saharan Africa. In size and shape, it resembles the Common Buzzard. Early in the year before wasps and bees are active, birds will often feed on frogs and newts by snatching them out of shallow water. The usual hunting technique is 'still hunting,' waiting for foraging wasps. They will follow the wasps back to their nests; if the nest has been built in the open, the entire nest may be taken. Otherwise the buzzards will dig with their feet anywhere up to a depth of 16in (40cm) to expose the nest.

MAKING A BEELINE

Western Honey Buzzards (*Pernis apivorus*) breed late in the year so that the juvenile birds start to fledge just as wasps and bees are most abundant to provide them with a source of food. Shortly after fledging, they will migrate, sometimes covering distances in excess of 6000 miles (10,000km). The juvenile birds have much paler bodies than the adults, often with a white head and darker wings. They lose their juvenile plumage at their first molt.

Harriers

There are 13 species of harrier. These birds are predominantly hunters of marsh and wetland regions, though they are found in many drier open localities, such as the pampas prairies of South America.

Harriers characteristically have long, slender wings, a long tail, and long legs. Their preferred method of hunting is by quartering their hunting territory with long gliding flights, to which their wings are ideally suited. Their long legs remain hanging low during these gliding flights in readiness to grab any prey quickly by surprise.

All harriers have a pronounced facial ruff, which indicates a significant reliance on sound to locate prey in the reeds and long grass that grow in the areas in which they hunt. They are often considered the diurnal counterparts of the short-eared owl family that frequently live and hunt in the same regions at night.

Harriers mainly prey on small wetland wading birds, small mammals, amphibians, reptiles, and large insects. In some regions the birds concentrate on particular prey that is present in abundance. Wintering in Africa, both the Pallid Harrier and Montagu's Harrier may feed there principally on migratory locusts.

OMNIVORE

The African Gymnogene (*Polyboroides typus*), or African Harrier-Hawk, enjoys a very varied diet. As well as eggs, young birds, frogs and other reptiles, insects, small mammals, and the occasional bat, they will often feed on oil-palm nuts. To reach the nuts, the bird carefully walks along the palm fronds steadying itself with its wings, appearing almost to use them to hold on. When the African Gymnogene is threatened, is hunting, or is in courtship displays, its bare face can rapidly change color from pale yellow to deep red.

With the exception of the Spotted Harrier from Australia, which nests in trees, harriers nest on the ground, often building fairly flimsy structures that are hidden amongst reeds or other vegetation. The females take on most of the responsibility for incubating the eggs and protecting the young in the first weeks after hatching. Despite needing up to seven weeks from hatching before they are fully fledged, the young often start straying from the nest at around two weeks because the nests are on the ground.

Closely related to the harriers are the African and Madagascar Gymnogenes or harrier-hawks. Similar in size to harriers, they are somewhat lighter with broader wings. In flight they are much more buoyant, making them look rather butterfly-like when in the air.

They take a very large variety of prey, often hunting on the ground. Eggs and young birds nesting in hollows of trees are particular targets. They will climb up to the nesting hole and reach inside it, taking advantage of the fact that their legs are double-jointed so they can bend in both directions to assist in finding food.

True Hawks

This group of raptors consists of 61 species, of which 47 belong to the Accipiter family, often referred to as true hawks.

Most of the Accipiters are woodland or scrubland hunting birds. Their short, broad, strong wings are suited to dashing between trees with great acceleration. Their long tails help them to change direction quickly to follow their prey as they dart between the trees.

The majority of these hawks prey on small to medium-sized birds, usually caught in flight after a brief dashing flight from a 'still hunting' perch. Other prey includes large insects, reptiles, and small mammals.

The largest of the true hawks is the Northern Goshawk, which weighs up to 5lb (2.3kg). It is found through much of the northern hemisphere. In the North American continent it is most often seen in Alaska and Canada and the northern and western states of the USA. It rarely appears in the southeastern states. In addition to medium-sized game birds, gulls, and waders, it also preys on a number of other raptors including the Honey Buzzard in Europe and many species of owl. It will catch mammals such as rabbits and both ground and tree squirrels. A ferocious hunter, sturdily built with very powerful legs, it can often catch and kill prey larger and heavier than itself.

The smallest of the true hawks is the Little Sparrowhawk, which weighs a mere 4oz (113g). It is found in southern and western Africa. In addition to smaller birds and mammals, these raptors will also prey on bats.

Most hawks build their own nests, though some will modify the disused nests of other birds. The nests are generally situated high up in trees. The average clutch sizes for hawks are between three and six eggs. The female looks after most of the incubation of the eggs. After hatching, the male is initially responsible for supplying the food for both the young and the female. As the young grow in size and require more nourishment, then the female will also help in providing food. The female is able to catch bigger prey because it is much larger than the male.

NOBLE HAWK

The name Goshawk derives from the Anglo-Saxon name of 'Goose Hawk.' The Northern Goshawk (*Accipiter gentilis*) is the largest of the true hawks or Accipiters and is a powerful, aggressive hunting bird. In Medieval England only noble men were allowed to own a Goshawk, which explains why the bird's scientific name is derived from the Latin words for noble (*'gentiles'*) and hawk (*'accipiter'*).

KITING

Red-backed Hawks (*Buteo polyosoma*) hunt mainly from the air. By kiting into the wind they are able to maintain their position with very few wing beats, as they scan the ground for small mammals, mainly cavies. If no prey is spotted, they will glide on for a short distance and then resume their wind hovering. When a target is spotted, they stoop directly down upon their prey.

PERCH AND POUNCE

Above: Red-shouldered Hawks (*Buteo lineatus*) generally live in damp, deciduous woodland, often close to water and swamps. They generally use a 'perch and pounce' style of hunting – searching for prey while perched on a treetop, then dropping on to it from the air. They feed on a wide variety of reptiles, amphibians, and small mammals and occasionally fish, crayfish, and small birds.

NO WAY IN

Right: Even the very powerful feet of the Galapagos Hawk (*Buteo galapagoensis*) are incapable of breaking through the shells of adult tortoises. They are indigenous to the Galapagos Islands off the west coast of Ecuador and feed mainly on giant centipedes and locusts, although they will occasionally take hatchling tortoises and young iguanas.

SUMMER HOLIDAY

Red Kites (*Milvus milvus*) are found through much of mainland Europe from the southern tip of Sweden down to the south of Spain and Italy. The more northerly birds migrate south over winter, while young birds usually remain in the warmer regions for their first summer, migrating back to their wintering regions in their second year.

FAIR GAME

Northern Goshawks (*Accipiter gentilis*) sometimes prey on larger game birds, such as pheasants and grouse, but they are more likely to catch smaller birds, such as thrushes, starlings and pigeons. A single Woodpigeon provides sufficient food for a Goshawk for a day. Unfortunately, they are still persecuted in some areas because of the threat they are thought to pose to game birds.

FALCONS

The falcons are the kings of speed of the raptor world. The Peregrine Falcon is on record as achieving the fastest speed of any animal. Excluding caracaras, there are currently 54 known different species of falcon, consisting of 39 species of true falcons plus pygmy falcons, falconets, forest-falcons, and the Laughing Falcon.

The smallest of the falcon family is the sparrow-sized Black-thighed Falconet found in Indonesia and Malaya, which weighs between 1 and 2oz (28-56g). The largest is the Gyr Falcon. This is found during summer above the Arctic Circle, while it winters as far down as the US/Canadian border and northern Scandinavia. Female Gyr Falcons may weigh anywhere up to 4.5lb (2kg).

The word falcon derives from the Latin word 'falco' meaning scimitar-shaped – a reference to the shape of their wings. Falcons have long narrow wings, which are swept back from the body enabling them to fly very fast.

In addition to the characteristic wings, most falcons have a notch in the upper beak. Called the 'tomial tooth,' there are suggestions that this may be a vestigial tooth left over from their reptilian ancestry. If their prey is not killed outright by their attack, falcons will administer a final *coup de grâce* by biting the victim's neck. The notch is ideally suited to fitting around and breaking the neck of small prey.

Most falcons also have a dark strip of feathers below the eyes extending downward from the beak, looking somewhat like a mustache. Known as the 'malar strip,' these dark feathers reduce the effect of glare in the birds' eyes.

Unlike many other birds of prey, falcons rarely eat carrion, preferring freshly caught prey. They rely both on speed and agility to catch their prey, generally hunting smaller birds that are caught in flight. Many falcons have an elongated middle toe, which is often used to help grasp prey while in flight.

Falcons rely on several strategies to catch their prey. Kestrels, in particular, use hovering and stooping as their preferred hunting method. Another technique is to use low-level chasing, rising at the last moment to catch the prey from above. The method of predation that most people associate with falcons is the strike from above – they gain great height and then stoop from altitude and hit the prey at high speed.

When stooping in this way, falcons use thermals to gain height and then soar in search of their prey. Once it is located, they drop down toward it, often using powered flight (flapping their wings) to increase their speed, and at the last moment they level off to strike the prey at high speed, usually from behind. Some falcons will approach their prey

HOVER CRAFT

Left: The Common Kestrel (*Falco tinnunculus*) is the only bird of prey that can perform a sustained true hover – remaining motionless above the ground using flapping motions of its wings to maintain its position, even in still air. Along with other raptors, its preferred method is 'wind hovering' – facing into the wind with wings and tail set at the correct angle to remain stationary aloft with minimal flapping.

THE TRAIL'S TALE

Below: When leaving their nests for food, voles mark their trail with urine, which is highly reflective of ultraviolet light. Common Kestrels are able to see well into the ultraviolet spectrum and, hovering above, the vole's bright tell-tale trail enables the Kestrel to locate its prey with ease.

with their toes bunched tight like fists, and held close to the body, punching out at the target as they pass. Other falcons will approach the prey with their feet facing forward, striking it with the base of the foot. This has the effect of bending the foot around so that the rear talon rakes through the prey, sometimes taking the head clean off smaller prey. Whichever technique is used, within a fraction of a second of the strike falcons are able to grasp the prey with their elongated toes. On the occasions when they miss an outright kill, they will chase the prey down, often catching it before it hits the ground. If not already dead, it will be despatched with a quick nip to the neck.

The smallest members of the falcon family, pygmy falcons and falconets, are found in parts of Africa, India, China, and the Indo-Malayan regions. They have the notched beak and elongated toes that are characteristic of the main falcon family, but they are only capable of catching much smaller prey. While these little raptors will feed on small birds, their diet also consists of insects, including butterflies, moths, and dragonflies. Occasionally they catch small reptiles and mammals. Rather than using the high-flying and stooping techniques of hunting, they usually perch above the ground waiting for their prey and then quickly dart out when it is spotted.

SPEED KILLS

Mainly catching birds in flight, Peregrine Falcons (*Falco peregrinus*) are capable of killing prey over twice their own weight. The sheer speed at which they strike their prey will often kill it outright. Here, a Peregrine Falcon is seen on a dead pheasant.

South America is home to some far less typical members of the falcon family, the forest-falcons and the Laughing Falcon. Living and hunting in forested areas, their wings tend to be shorter than those of the true falcons. Their toes also tend to be shorter and they all lack the characteristic notched beak. These latter variations reflect differences in their prey. Like some owls and harriers, forest-falcons have a slight facial ruff, which may indicate that they rely on sound to locate their prey to a greater degree than true falcons do.

Forest-falcons feed on a variety of prey, much like the buzzard (buteo) family. The diet includes most small prey animals that abound in tropical forests, including lizards, insects and beetles, frogs, small birds, and crabs. Forest-falcons use a variety of hunting techniques including 'still hunting,' 'perch hunting,' and foraging on the ground looking for prey. Two species, the Slaty-backed Forest-Falcon and the Collared Forest-Falcon, are thought to have a special call which is difficult to locate but which induces a mobbing response in small birds. This reaction allows them to locate their prey easily.

The Laughing Falcon preys predominantly on snakes of both harmless and venomous varieties. It mainly uses 'still hunting' to catch its prey. As the snake passes, it will pounce down and catch the snake behind the head with its feet and then render the snake harmless by biting off its head. The snake will be eaten on a feeding perch, rather

IT'S ALL IN THE TIMING

Most falcons catch their prey from behind, but the Lanner Falcon (*Falco biamarcus*) will regularly attack its prey head on. As the relative approach speed between falcon and prey is greatly increased by this tactic, exceptional agility and timing are required by the Lanner to ensure a clean strike and kill.

ON THE LEDGE

The Peregrine Falcon's (*Falco peregrinus*) favored nesting site is on the steep sides of cliffs. Sometimes they use a simple 'scrape' on bare rock as a nest, although they will often occupy the disused nest of a different bird. In urban areas, Peregrines select balconies on skyscrapers, ledges on churches and cathedrals, and crevices in tall chimneys as suitable nesting sites.

than on the ground; smaller snakes will be carried in the beak, larger snakes in the feet.

Falcons almost never build nests of their own. Many take over the disused nests of other birds. Some lay their eggs in small scrapes on cliff ledges; others use hollows in trees. Some falcons that live close to man-made structures will use those too. There have been many reports in recent years of Peregrine Falcons nesting on the tops of tall buildings, such as skyscrapers, in very close proximity to people. In Britain and Europe, the Common Kestrel regularly hunts along the verges and central reservations of freeways. They have even been found nesting in structures located along the freeways, including roadsigns. Due to the bird's protected status in the UK, a pair of Common Kestrels even brought major road repair work to a halt for several months by nesting underneath a freeway bridge.

The average clutch size of a falcon ranges from three to five eggs, though some will only lay a single egg while clutches of up to nine have been recorded for some species. The eggs are normally laid at two- to three-day intervals. The female mainly looks after incubation, and for most species this lasts in the region of four to five weeks. The young are fully fledged anywhere from four to eight weeks after hatching.

While some young birds are dependent on their parents for a few weeks after fledging, others, such as the Lesser Kestrel, may only be dependent for about one week. One instance has been recorded of full independence in only two days! At the other end of the spectrum, the young of the Seychelles Kestrel may remain dependent on their parents for nearly six months after fledging.

Once they achieve independence, most young will stay in the region of the nest site for up to a month. However some, like young Barbary Falcons which are fully independent eight weeks after hatching, may stay with their parents for a further three months. During this period it is not unusual for groups of juvenile birds to form social hunting groups. Where stooping is a favored method of hunting, the young will often accompany the parent birds which catch small prey and then fly above the young and drop the prey in order to encourage the stooping behavior in their offspring.

FAST LEARNERS, BIG EATERS

In the first few weeks of life, young Peregrine Falcons are completely dependent on their parents for food. Usually the male will provide prey, which will be fed to the young by the female. As the young birds grow, both parents may need to hunt to provide sufficient food for them. Fledging can take place at around five to six weeks, when the parents will start to teach the young to hunt for themselves.

LOCAL PRODUCE

With only limited food sources to be found in the Arctic region, Gyr Falcons (*Falco rusticolus*) must rely on what is available locally. In some regions the diet consists mainly of birds from the size of small finches to large geese and Capercaillie. In other regions the food is predominantly mammals, including voles, hares, and lemmings. Ground-hugging chases over several miles may be required to catch some fast-moving prey.

A CHANGE OF STYLE

Above: American Kestrel (*Falco sparverius*) and right: Common Kestrel (*Falco tinnunculus*). Hovering in flight to hunt consumes a lot of energy, so kestrels will often prefer 'still hunting' from a high perch, followed by a drop and glide to catch their prey. Kestrels eat small mammals, as well as a variety of ground-based prey including insects, beetles, and earthworms. Once commonly known as the Sparrow Hawk because of its small stature (it is only 7.5-10.5in [19-27cm] in length), the American Kestrel is actually a true falcon. Unlike most falcons, however, they take relatively few birds in flight as prey.

GO SOUTH, YOUNG BIRD

Opposite: Young Merlins (*Falco columbarius*) usually take their first flight within four weeks of hatching, and their flying skills develop rapidly. Merlins breed throughout northern Europe, Asia, and North America. Around six weeks after fledging, they will set out on their long migration south for the winter.

BETWEEN THE TREES

Right: The wings of the Lined Forest-Falcon (*Micrastur gilvicollis*) are much more rounded than those of most other falcons, which are generally pointed. They are well adapted to hunting in forests, and the birds appear to prefer a woodland habitat, flying around the edges of trees, rather than across open ground. Very often they will hunt on foot, catching small mammals on the ground, rather than chasing small birds in flight.

HOODWINKED

Peregrine Falcon (*Falco peregrinus*). Most of the predators of falcons are nocturnal, and they rely mainly on sound to locate their prey while they roost at night. The falconer's habit of using a hood to control his falcons stems from the raptor's natural instinct to be still and quiet in the dark, so that it may remain safe from predators. They are hoodwinked by the falconer into thinking it is night time during the day.

VULTURES

These birds are Nature's sanitation workers. They are predominantly carrion eaters, picking clean dead carcasses before they begin to rot and potentially create a health hazard. In addition to feeding on carrion, many are also scavengers and are consequently often found near population centers, feeding on garbage tips that are often situated at the edge of towns.

There are two groups of vultures: the new world vultures found in North and South America and the old world vultures found in Africa, Asia, and Europe. The provide an excellent example of what is known as 'convergent evolution:' despite many similarities, such as diet and their bald heads and necks, the two groups are unrelated. New world vultures are more closely related to storks and herons than to any of the members of the raptor family.

The vultures are the oldest of the diurnal raptors. Fossil records of new world vultures date back to some 50 million years ago and those of old world vultures to around 30 million years ago. Fossils of both old and new world vultures have been found in Europe and the Americas. Why the new world vultures became extinct in Europe and the old world vultures became extinct in the Americas is, to this day, a mystery.

One of the major differences between the two groups can be seen in their feet. New world vultures have much smaller feet, more suited to

NOT SO DIRTY BUZZARD

Along with other vultures, the Turkey Vulture (*Cathartes aura*), or Turkey Buzzard, has the reputation of being a dirty bird. Even though their diet is carrion, they prefer not to eat rotten flesh, however, concentrating mainly on the fresher parts. After feeding, they usually bathe and often spend up to three hours preening themselves.

PREVIOUS PAGES

Page 66: The brightly colored King Vulture (*Sarcorhamphus papa*).
Page 67: The Lappet-faced Vulture (*Aegypius tracheliotus*) is an old world vulture that lives in central and southern Africa.

walking than to killing. Despite rarely killing with them, old world vultures' feet are much more similar to those of other raptors.

New World Vultures

There are seven species of new world vulture: the Andean Condor, the Californian Condor, the King Vulture, the Black Vulture, the Turkey Vulture, and the Greater and Lesser Yellow-headed Vultures.

The Andean Condor may be ranked as the largest of all flying birds. While the Maribou Stork and the Wandering Albatross both have slightly larger wingspans, the Andean Condor is much heavier than either. The Californian Condor comes a very close second to the Andean Condor in terms of both wingspan and weight.

Condors only breed every other year. The female Andean Condor lays two eggs whereas the Californian Condor only lays a single egg. The eggs are usually laid on the ground amongst boulders or in hollows on mountain cliffs or remote ledges. These 'nests' are normally situated close to large trees where the adults can roost. The young stay in the 'nests' for around 20 weeks, but then spend the next seven months running around on the ground before they are able to fly and hunt for

themselves. They are dependent on the parent birds for up to another seven months. Condors take around five to six years to mature into fully developed adults.

Other than the King Vulture, which lays its eggs in crevices in trees, other new world vultures also lay their eggs directly on the ground, usually on cliff ledges which are fairly inaccessible to other animals.

By the early 1980s, the population of Californian Condors had dwindled to 21 known birds, both wild and in captivity. Since then a captive breed and release program has significantly increased the wild population, but it is still far from being secure.

Unlike other birds of prey, Turkey Vultures (and to a much lesser extent, the Greater and Lesser Yellow-headed Vultures) have a very keen sense of smell. They are able to detect a dead carcass from several miles away, long before it starts to rot. Other vultures will often rely on the Turkey Vulture's sense of smell, watching the skies for groups of Turkey Vultures to start circling above a carcass. Once spotted, they will quickly fly to the carcass and chase off the Turkey Vultures. When a large carcass has been found, many types of scavenger will arrive, and a distinct 'pecking' order is observed: eagles and coyotes get the first share, condors next and last in line are the Turkey Vultures and ravens.

With the exception of the Greater and Lesser Yellow-headed Vultures, new world vultures are very gregarious birds. It is not unusual to see groups of up to 200 Black Vultures and Turkey Vultures all feeding together, and groups of over 1000 Black Vultures roosting together.

New world vultures lack a syrinx, the vocal organ used by birds, and so they are voiceless and can only produce faint hissing and grunts by way of sound.

Old World Vultures

There are 15 species of old world vulture found across southern Europe, Africa, the Middle East, and much of Asia. The largest of these is the Monk Vulture, comparable in size to Californian Condors. The smallest is the Hooded Vulture, which is about the size of a raven.

As they are closer relatives of modern diurnal raptors than the new world vultures, the feet of old world vultures are much more suited to grabbing prey. Despite this adaptation, however, with one exception they rarely use their feet to kill their prey, relying mainly on scavenging or feeding on carrion. The exception is the Lappet-faced Vulture, which regularly catches live prey, such as small mammals, and even birds as large as flamingos.

One of the old world vultures – the Palmnut Vulture – is unique amongst birds of prey. While it will eat molluscs, crabs, small mammals, insects, and some carrion, it much prefers a vegetarian diet. Some other

SOCIAL VULTURE

The Black Vulture (*Coragyps atratus*) is the smallest of the new world vultures. Far more social than the slightly larger Turkey Vulture, groups of over 200 have been seen feeding together, with groups of over 1000 sometimes roosting in the same area.

VEGETARIAN CHOICE

A predominantly nut-eating raptor, the Palmnut Vulture (*Gypohierax angolensis*) was once thought to be closely related to the fish eagles. The other common name by which it is known is the Vulturine Fish Eagle, indicating the difficulty ornithologists have had in classifying this bird.

birds of prey do eat small amounts of vegetable matter and grass, but this is the only raptor that relies on fruit, especially the husks of oil palm nuts and raphia fruit, as its staple diet.

Another very large vulture, the Lammergeier, feeds mainly on the bones of carcasses that it finds. Up to 85 percent of its diet can be bones, and if Lammergeiers are unable to crack the bones with their beaks, they will fly high in the sky with the bones and drop them onto the rocks below in order to smash the bones open.

None of the old world vultures has a sense of smell and so they are all dependent on their eyesight to locate their prey. Some vultures, such as Rüppell's Vulture, like to search out thermals and gain height to soar around the skies searching either for their food or to spot other carnivores feeding on a carcass. Others, such as the Egyptian Vulture, prefer low-level flight, quartering out their territory in a style similar to harriers.

Unlike new world vultures, old world vultures all make nests. Usually the nests are quite small to begin with, and they are made from sticks and branches, often lined with grass and dung. When first made, the parent bird frequently dwarfs the nests. The nests tend to be reused in subsequent years, usually being added to and relined. Over a number of years the nests can grow quite large.

Some vultures, such as the White-backed Vulture and the White-rumped Vulture, choose to build their nests in high trees, while others prefer to build their nests on cliff edges. Occasionally, some Himalayan Vultures will take over the nests made in previous years by Lammergeiers, rather than building their own.

As with new world vultures, the clutch size is very small, usually one egg, sometimes two, and very rarely three. Most of the young are fully fledged by about four months after hatching, but some remain dependent on their parents for a further three to four months. The young of the Lammergeier remain dependent on their parents for anywhere up to a year. Many vultures are very gregarious birds, and the young will often stay in the same colonies as the parent birds.

A CREATURE OF HABIT

The Monk Vulture (*Aegypius monachus*), also known as the Cinerous or Black Vulture, is the largest of the old world vultures. Often arriving late at a carcass, they are large enough to dominate and drive off numbers of other smaller vultures that may be feeding.

GREGARIOUS GRIFFONS

Left: Rüppell's Vulture (*Gyps rueppellii*) and above: Griffon Vulture (*Gyps fulvus*). These closely related vultures were previously referred to simply as Griffons – Rüppell's Griffon and the European Griffon. Family members are characterized by their very long necks, highly suited for delving deep into the body of carcasses, and the thick ruffs of feathers at the neckline. They are very gregarious vultures – large groups feed and roost together, often as mixed groups where the territories of different species overlap.

WHEN NIGHT FALLS

Once paired, Hooded Vultures (*Necrosyrtes monachus*) appear to be devoted to each other. Often remaining close to their nesting site, they will commonly roost together in the evenings even outside the breeding season. Their nests are built in trees, carefully lined with fresh greenery during the nesting season, and reused in subsequent years.

A single egg is laid, and the female spends most of her time sitting protectively on it, while being fed by her mate. The young are very weak when they are hatched, and require considerably more parental attention than do most other vulture young.

OWLS

Owls are often referred to as nocturnal raptors to distinguish them from the diurnal raptors, but the description is not entirely accurate. With very few exceptions, diurnal raptors prefer to hunt during daylight, relying mainly on sight to locate their prey. The owl family includes species that span the day in the times that they prefer to hunt, relying on both sight and sound to locate their prey.

Completely unrelated to all diurnal birds of prey, they are another example of 'convergent evolution.' Fossil records date owls back to around 50 million years ago, which makes them contemporaries of the new world vultures. Of all the other species of bird, owls are most closely related to nightjars.

The owl family ranges in size from the very small Elf Owls, Least Pygmy Owls, and Long-whiskered Owlets that are around the size of sparrows and weigh around 1.5oz (43g), up to the magnificent Eurasian Eagle Owl, which is a heavily built, broad-winged bird that weighs up to 9lb (4.1kg) and has a wing span of over 6ft (2m).

With the exception of the Antarctic and the Sahara desert, owls are found throughout the world living and hunting in all types of terrain. The widest ranging of all the owls is the familiar Barn Owl, found throughout North and South America, Europe, most of Africa, India, parts of Asia, and all of Australia.

TWO-WIT TWO-OOO

The Tawny Owl (*Strix aluco*) is very vocal, and adults use eight to ten different basic calls. Most famously, this is the owl that makes the classic 'twit-two-ooo' call. Often this call is really made by a pair of owls, as the female starts with a 'ke-wick' call, which is followed very quickly by the male's 'hoooo.'

PREVIOUS PAGES

Page 76: Young Snowy Owl (*Bubo scandiacus*).

Page 77: Long-eared Owl (*Asio otus*).

What really distinguishes owls from the diurnal birds of prey is their hearing. Below the feathers on their heads, roughly level with their eyes, their ears are arranged asymmetrically: one ear being slightly higher than the other. This asymmetry, coupled with side-to-side and twisting movements of the head, gives them the ability to locate sources of sound very accurately. While owls have eyesight that is much better than ours in low levels of light at night, they cannot see in total darkness, but instead locate and catch their prey by sound alone.

The shape of the face is a very good indicator of how much owls rely on sound to locate their prey. The beak and the ridge of stiff feathers surrounding it reflect sound back to the dish-shaped face, which in turn acts rather like an ear trumpet channeling the sound directly to the ears. The Great Gray Owl has the most pronounced dish-shaped face of all of the owls. Spending much of the year living on the edge of the Arctic tundra, it is quite capable of catching small mammals burrowing under 18in (46cm) of snow, locating them by the sounds that they make as they move. The owls with perhaps the least well defined facial disk are those like the Brown Fish Owl which rely on sight to locate their staple prey of fish.

Even during daylight, owls often rely on the sound that their prey makes. When in flight, owls' wings are directly level with their ears. As they often hunt small prey that make hardly any sound, they would lose their ability to locate their prey if their wingbeats were noisy. Consequently, owls have evolved to have completely silent flight. The wing feathers of owls are much softer than those of other birds of prey, and the feathers on the leading edges of the wings have very fine serrations. Both of these adaptations allow some of the air to flow through the feathers, rather than over them, so reducing the noise made by air rushing over the wings. This noiseless flight means that owls can approach their prey in total silence, often catching the victim completely unaware that it is being hunted.

Owls have very large eyes, but lack muscles to move them in the eye sockets. As the eyes are forward-facing, this gives the bird no rearward view. To compensate for this, owls have adapted in two ways. Firstly, they have extra neck vertebrae which allow them both to turn their head much further round and also to be able to twist and tilt it further than other animals. Secondly, the muscles in their necks are very strong, permitting them to twist their heads from one side to the other very quickly. It is the combination of the two adaptations that makes it seem as if an owl can turn its head all the way round from the forward-facing position. In fact, no owl can do this. From the forward-facing position most species of owl can turn their heads at least 180 degrees to look

LOOK INTO MY EYES

As a group, owls hunt throughout the day and night, with individual species specializing at particular times. The eye coloration usually gives a good indication of the preferred time of hunting for the species. Left, above: Yellow-eyed owls, such as the Great Horned Owl (*Bubo virginianus*) prefer to hunt during the daytime. Left, below: Orange-eyed owls like the Indian Eagle Owl (*Bubo bengalensis*) prefer to hunt at dusk and dawn. Above: Dark-eyed owls like this Brown Wood Owl (*Strix leptogrammica*) are generally night-time hunters.

straight behind while the Great Horned Owl is able to turn its head 270 degrees, three-quarters of the way round a full circle. From the furthest extremity in one direction, they are able to turn their heads all the way to the opposite extremity so quickly that it is barely noticeable.

Owls feed on a variety of prey including mammals, insects, reptiles, bats, and birds. Some nocturnal owls will regularly take roosting diurnal raptors. Depending on species, the prey mammals range in size from mice and shrews up to rabbits. Some are even larger than that. A large female Eurasian Eagle Owl is capable of killing a small adult sheep or a roe deer, though this is unusual. Some owls have more specialist diets. Fish owls, as their name suggests, mainly take fish. Others have a more limited diet simply due to the regions they inhabit. For example, the population level of Snowy Owls in the Arctic is known to reflect that of a favored prey, the lemming. In years when lemmings are plentiful, the population of Snowy Owls is high and migration is slow. In years when the lemming population is low, the Snowy Owls migrate very early in search of food.

WHO, ME?

Above: The large head and comparatively small eyes and beak give the Northern Saw-whet Owl (*Aegolius acadicus*) a permanent look of surprise. Its call, sounding very much like a saw being sharpened, gives it its name. At dusk and dawn they hunt for mice, shrews, and voles, and will often catch several in quick succession without eating them, hiding them in safe places to eat later when prey is less abundant.

BIG BIRD

Right: The Eurasian Eagle Owl (*Bubo bubo*) is the largest of all the owl family. Females can weigh anywhere up to 9lb (4.1kg) and have a wingspan of up to 79in (2m). They are active mainly from dusk to dawn. A Eurasian Eagle Owl's flight is noiseless, and soft wingbeats are interspersed with periods of gliding when they are flying over long distances.

Owls nest in a variety of places, such as in holes in trees, on cliff edges, or in hollows in the ground. The Burrowing Owl even nests underground in disused burrows made by prairie dogs and squirrels. They rarely build their own nests, preferring to use nests abandoned by other birds. Owls frequently try to use the same nest sites year after year.

Owls tend to have only a single partner, but they do not always mate for life. The partnership very often only lasts for a single breeding season. The number of eggs that are laid varies between species; anywhere from one to 15 eggs may be laid. In species that lay large numbers of eggs, the number produced in any year is often directly related to the available supply of food. The eggs are laid over a period of days, but incubation starts immediately. This means that the eggs also hatch over a corresponding period of days. The young that hatch first tend have an advantage over their younger siblings, being larger and stronger. They often get the majority of the food and sometimes will even kill the younger nestlings. The surviving chicks usually eat any dead chicks in the nest.

Owls are fully fledged anywhere between four to ten weeks after hatching, the smaller owls often fledging earlier than larger owls. They reach their full adult size at around three to four months of age, and will be fully independent of their parents shortly afterward.

WELL CAMOUFLAGED

The female Snowy Owl (*Bubo scandiacus*) is responsible for incubation of the eggs and early rearing of the young. Nesting on the ground in open areas of the Arctic tundra, in shallow scrapes made by her talons, the strong dark markings on the female help keep her camouflaged while she is on the nest. Nest sites are located near plentiful hunting areas. They must be snow-free, and high enough to command a good view of the surrounding terrain.

BIG PREY, SMALL PREY

Left and above: With their massive and powerful feet, Eurasian Eagle Owls (*Bubo bubo*) can kill animals as large as sheep or roe deer. They usually only do this in times of severe food shortage and generally prey on much smaller mammals, such as rabbits, hares, and even hedgehogs. They will also forage on the ground for small insects and earthworms.

FAIR SHARES

Eurasian Eagle Owls need large open spaces in which to hunt. They have been known to share hunting areas amicably with other raptors, such as Golden Eagles, as the owls hunt from dusk through to dawn, and the eagles hunt during the daytime. Eurasian Eagle Owls have been recorded as living for more than 60 years in captivity. In the wild, their average lifespan is about 20 years. They have no real natural predators and the main causes of death are electrocution from power cables, collision with traffic, and shooting.

WINTER COAT

Left: A Great Gray Owl (*Strix nebulosa*). Despite looking bulky, the Great Gray Owl's body is actually relatively small. Much of its apparent size is due to the dense, but light, feathers covering its head and body, which provide excellent insulation against the cold. It preys on small mammals up to the size of rabbits.

TAKE HEART

Above: Barn Owls (*Tyto alba*) are common around the world, being found on all continents with the exception of the Antarctic. Barn Owls and their close relatives, Grass Owls, all have very distinctive heart-shaped faces.

PHANTOM OF THE NIGHT

In bright moonlight pale colored Barn Owls stand out very clearly against the dark night sky. With gentle beats of their softly-feathered wings, interspersed with short glides, they fly silently and disappear into the darkness, seeming almost ghost-like.

WISE OLD OWL

With relatively large eyes and ears
that can occupy over half of their
small skulls, owls have fairly small
brains. The story of the 'wise old owl'
stems from Ancient Greek mythology.
A Little Owl (*Athene noctua*) was a
constant companion to Athene, the
goddess of wisdom, and was
considered sacred. Large numbers of
Little Owls traditionally nested on the
Acropolis in Athens, where the temple
of Athene is found.

WINTER BOOTS

All raptors rely on their feet to catch
their prey. Any injury to their feet will
hamper the bird in its quest for food
and it may eventually starve to death
as a consequence. The Snowy Owl
(*Bubo scandiacus*) has the most
heavily feathered feet of all birds of
prey, as protection against the
extreme Arctic cold.

LOW-LEVEL HUNTER

Below: Found across the northern hemisphere and the southern portion of South America, Short-eared Owls (*Asio flammeus*) migrate to the tropics during winter. They prefer to inhabit wide open areas, hunting mainly for small mammals. Prey is normally located by low-level quartering flights over their chosen territory.

TREE HUGGER

Opposite: Long-eared owls (*Asio otus*) are almost completely nocturnal in their hunting habits. During the day, they roost on branches of trees. When approached by a possible predator, a Long-eared Owl will hug close to the tree, stretching its body and wrapping a wing round the trunk to blend in with the bark and camouflage itself. The 'ear' tufts of varying lengths which can be seen on many owls have nothing to do with hearing. These long feathers are used partly for camouflage, partly for communication, and also to attract a mate.

INDEX

African Gymnogene (*Polyboroides typus*) 40

American Kestrel (*Falco sparverius*) 50, 60

Andean Condor (*Vultur gryphus*) 68

Baby Falcon 57

Bald Eagle (*Haliaeetus leucocephalus*) 1, 14, 16, 18, 19, 28

Barn Owl (*Tyto alba*) 76, 87, 88

Black Kite (*Milvus migrans*) 36

Black Vulture (*Coragyps atratus*) 68, 69

Brown Wood Owl (*Strix leptogrammica*) 79

Burrowing Owl (*Athene cunicularia*) 81

Californian Condor (*Gymnogyps californianus*) 68

Common Buzzard (*Buteo buteo*) 32

Common Kestrel (*Falco tinnunculus*) 53, 56, 61

Crested Caracara (*Caracara plancus*) 12

Egyptian Vulture (*Neophron percnopterus*) 70

Eurasian Eagle Owl (*Bubo bubo*) 76, 80, 82, 83, 84

Ferruginous Hawk (*Buteo regalis*) 32

Forster's Caracara (*Phalcoboenus australis*) 12, 13

Galapagos Hawk (*Buteo galapagoensis*) 45

Golden Eagle (*Aquila chrysaetos*) 15, 18, 22, 23

Great Gray Owl (*Strix nebulosa*) 78, 86

Great Horned Owl (*Bubo virginianus*) 79, 80

Griffon Vulture (*Gyps fulvus*) 73

Gyr Falcon (*Falco rusticolus*) 50, 58

Harpy Eagle (*Harpia harpyja*) 19, 20

Harris' Hawk (*Parabuteo unicinctus harrisi*) 34

Hen Harrier (*Circus cyaneus*) 39

Hooded Vulture (*Necrosyrtes monachus*) 69, 74

Imperial Eagle (*Aquila heliaca*) 24

Indian Eagle Owl (*Bubo bengalensis*) 79

King Vulture (*Sarcoramphus papa*) 66, 68

Lammergeier (*Gypaetus barbatus*) 70

Lanner Falcon (*Falco biamarcus*) 55

Lappet-faced Vulture (*Aegypius tracheliotus*) 67

Least Pygmy Owl (*Glaucidium minutissimum*) 76

Little Eagle (*Hieraaetus morphnoides*) 17

Little Owl (*Athene noctua*) 90

Lined Forest-falcon (*Micrastur gilvicollis*) 63

Long-eared Owl (*Asio otus*) 77, 95

Martial Eagle (*Polematus bellicosus*) 18

Merlin (*Falco columbarius*) 62

Monk Vulture (*Aegypius monachus*) 69, 71

Northern Goshawk (*Accipiter gentilis*) 41, 48

Northern Marsh Harrier (*Circus aeruginosus*) 38

Northern Saw-whet Owl (*Aegolius acadicus*) 80

Osprey (*Pandion haliaetus*) 7, 10, 20, 21, 30

Palmnut Vulture (*Gypohierax angolensis*) 8, 69, 70

Peregrine Falcon (*Falco peregrinus*) 50, 51, 54, 56, 64

Peregrine Falcon, African (*Falco peregrinus minor*) 52

Philippine Eagle (*Pithecophaga jeffreyi*) 17, 20

Red Kite (*Milvus milvus*) 35, 46

Red-backed Hawk (*Buteo polyosoma*) 42

Red-shouldered Hawk (*Buteo lineatus*) 44

Red-tailed Hawk (*Buteo jamaicensis*) 34

Roadside Hawk (*Rupornis magnirostris*) 32, 33

Rüppell's Vulture (*Gyps rueppellii*) 8, 70, 72

Secretarybird (*Sagittarius serpentarius*) 11

Short-eared Owl (*Asio flammeus*) 94

Short-toed Snake Eagle (*Circaetus gallicus*) 19

Snowy Owl (*Bubo scandiacus*) 2, 76, 80, 81, 92

Spotted Eagle Owl (*Bubo africanus*) 9

Spotted Harrier (*Circus assimilis*) 40

Steller's Fish Eagle (*Haliaeetus pelagicus*) 19

Tawny Eagle (*Aquila rapax*) 6

Tawny Eagle, Indian (*Aquila rapax vindhiana*) 17, 41

Tawny Owl (*Strix aluco*) 78

Turkey Vulture (*Cathartes aura*) 68

Wedge-tailed Eagle (*Aquila audax*) 26

Western Honey Buzzard (*Pernis apivorus*) 37

White-rumped Vulture (*Gyps bengalensis*) 71